# Sales Mastery

## Techniques for Building Relationships and Closing Deals

Isaac Wilson

# Table of Contents

# Sales Mastery

# Introduction

Sales mastery sets successful companies apart from the competition; it's more than just a skill. Learning the art of sales is essential to creating revenue development, cultivating client connections, and maintaining business success in today's cutthroat industry. This introduction summarizes the importance of sales expertise and delineates the main points of this book.

## Understanding the Value of Sales Mastery

Beyond just closing deals, sales expertise also entails establishing lasting connections, knowing the needs of customers, and effectively articulating value ideas. Sales mastery helps businesses remain flexible and responsive to market needs in a business climate that is becoming more and more dynamic as consumer preferences change quickly. Additionally, it gives salespeople the ability to seize opportunities, overcome obstacles, and adjust to changing conditions.

Additionally essential to generating cash is sales mastery. Organizations may improve sales performance and achieve sustainable growth by providing their sales personnel with the tactics, information, and skills necessary to flourish in their professions.

The key to increasing profitability and growing a firm is having a strong sales force, whether it is through bringing on new clients, upselling current ones, or entering untapped areas.

## Summary of the Book's Focus

The goal of this book is to give readers a thorough understanding of the concepts, methods, and recommended practices of sales mastery. It provides helpful advice for salespeople of all stripes, from novices looking to build fundamental abilities to seasoned veterans looking to improve their tactics. Readers will find practical tips, real-world examples, and tested tactics to improve their sales game and succeed beyond expectations in the highly competitive sales environment of today by paging through the chapters.

The next chapters explore many facets of sales proficiency, encompassing subjects like establishing a connection with clients, perfecting the sales procedure, utilizing technology to enhance sales efficiency, and much more. This book intends to empower people and companies to meet their sales goals, increase income, and prosper in a constantly changing business climate by giving readers the skills and information necessary to succeed in sales.

# Chapter 1: The Fundamentals of Sales

Any business depends on sales to generate money and expand, as they are the main engine of any enterprise. This section will cover the essential ideas and precepts of effective sales techniques, such as comprehending the basic function of sales in business, grasping the essential steps in the sales process, and developing the winning mentality.

## Defining Sales and Its Role in Business

The process of convincing prospective clients to buy the goods or services that a company is offering is known as sales. It entails determining the needs of the client, addressing those needs with solutions, and at the end, closing deals that satisfy the supplier and the buyer. Sales is more than just transactions; it's also about establishing rapport, finding solutions to issues, and providing clients with value.

Fundamentally, the goal of sales is to establish exchanges that benefit both parties and create value. Understanding the wants and motivations of customers and framing goods in a way that resonates with them are essential components of effective salesmanship, whether one is selling a tangible something, a service, or an idea.

Successful salespeople set themselves apart in today's cutthroat industry by offering individualized solutions and outstanding customer experiences in an environment where consumers have a plethora of options and easy access to information.

## Understanding the Sales Process: Prospecting, Qualifying, Presenting, Closing

Every stage of the sales process, which may be divided into multiple important ones, is essential to advancing prospects through the sales funnel and winning them over as clients. Typically, these phases include of qualifying, presenting, closing, and prospecting.

- Finding: Prospecting entails locating and vetting possible leads or prospects who might require the given goods or services. In order to find and get in touch with people or organizations who match the ideal client profile, this stage frequently calls for research, networking, and outreach initiatives.

- Eligibility: The following stage after identifying prospects is to qualify them to ascertain their degree of interest, requirements, and purchasing power. In order to qualify a prospect, you must probe them, evaluate their fit, and decide if they are a good fit for the offerings being made.

- Introducing: During the presentation phase, the value proposition of the good or service must be effectively and convincingly conveyed to the potential customer. This could entail making sales presentations, demonstrating products, and responding to any queries or objections that the prospect may have.

- Finishing: The sale actually happens at the closing stage. It entails addressing any lingering doubts, overcoming objections, and convincing the potential customer to make a purchase. Assumptive closes, direct requests for the sale, and trial closes are all effective closing strategies.

To succeed in sales, one must grasp every phase of the sales process. Sales professionals can successfully navigate the sales journey and assist prospects in making educated purchasing decisions by comprehending the dynamics of prospecting, qualifying, presenting, and closing.

## Building a Sales Mentality: Persistence, Resilience, and Confidence

Having the correct mindset is essential for success in sales, in addition to knowing the ins and outs of the sales process. Salespeople that possess a sales mindset are confident, resilient, and persistent, which helps them to overcome obstacles, recover from failures, and remain goal-focused.

- Assurance: Effective salesmanship is built on a foundation of confidence. It entails having faith in one's own abilities, worth of the offerings being made, and oneself. Salespeople that possess confidence are better able to establish rapport with prospects, project credibility, and radiate excitement and passion for their products.

- Adaptability: Rejection and setbacks are frequent in the sales industry, which can be a difficult and demanding job. The capacity to overcome adversity, rejection, and failure while retaining a positive mindset and perspective is known as resilience. Salespeople that are resilient see obstacles as chances for development and learning, and they persevere in the face of hardship and failure.

- Stability: The will to continue pursuing objectives in the face of hindrances, difficulties, and disappointments is known as persistence. It entails continuing to be dedicated to reaching sales targets, contacting prospects again, and being proactive in bringing in new business and leads. Salespeople who are persistent know that success frequently necessitates consistent effort and perseverance over an extended period of time.

Salespeople can surmount barriers, negotiate difficulties, and accomplish their goals more successfully by developing a sales mindset that is marked by assurance, resiliency, and willpower.

# Chapter 2: Building Rapport and Relationships

Successful salesmanship fundamentally involves building meaningful relationships with prospects and clients and building a strong rapport. This section will cover the craft of creating value propositions that appeal to consumers, developing effective communication techniques, and establishing trust.

## The Art of Building Trust with Prospects and Clients

Any successful business relationship is built on trust. Authenticity, moral rectitude, and a sincere desire to serve your clients' and prospects' best interests are necessary for developing trust. Salespeople can develop trust through:

- Authenticity: Acting sincere and open in their communications, exhibiting integrity and honesty in all of their dealings.

- Reliability: Regularly keeping word and fulfilling obligations, exhibiting dependability and reliability.

- Empathy: Showing empathy and understanding by being aware of the needs, worries, and viewpoints of prospects and clients.

- Competence: Exhibiting proficiency, understanding, and competence in addressing client needs and offering solutions.

- Consistency: Encouraging predictability and dependability by remaining consistent in behavior, communication, and service delivery.

Sales professionals can create enduring and mutually beneficial relationships with prospects and clients by emulating these traits and continuously exhibiting trustworthiness in their actions and interactions.

# Powerful Communication Techniques: Questioning, Empathy, and Listening

Establishing rapport and cultivating deep connections with prospects and clients requires effective communication. Salespeople can improve their ability to communicate by:

- Active Listening: Paying attention to the wants, needs, and worries of potential customers while exhibiting compassion and comprehension.

- Asking Questions: To learn more about the needs, preferences, and pain points of your customers and to develop a deeper understanding of their requirements, ask insightful and probing questions.

-         Empathetic         Communication: Acknowledging and validating the feelings of customers, speaking with empathy and sensitivity, and exhibiting sincere concern for their welfare.

- Clear and Concise Communication: Making sure that messages are easily understood and accessible to customers, as well as avoiding jargon and technical language.

Sales professionals can develop rapport, establish trust, and create lasting connections with prospects and clients by refining their communication skills and embracing a customer-centric approach to communication.

## Creating Value Propositions that Resonate with Customers

Gaining the interest and attention of potential customers requires a strong value proposition. Salespeople can craft value propositions that appeal to clients by:

- Understanding Customer Needs: Performing in-depth investigation and examination in order to comprehend the requirements, inclinations, and problems of the customer.

- Highlighting Benefits: Outlining in detail the special qualities and advantages of goods and services, as well as how they meet needs and resolve issues for clients.

- Differentiation: Highlighting what makes an offering stand out from rivals by identifying and conveying its competitive advantages and unique selling points.

- Tailoring Solutions: Adapting solutions to each customer's unique requirements and preferences while showcasing how offerings provide individualized value and advantages.

- Demonstrating ROI: Calculating the return on investment and putting the value proposition into concrete terms, like revenue growth, cost savings, or efficiency gains.

Sales professionals can effectively communicate the value of their offerings and set themselves apart in the marketplace by creating value propositions that are relevant, compelling, and customized to the needs and preferences of customers.

# Chapter 3: Prospecting and Lead Generation

Sales professionals can identify potential customers, build relationships, and eventually convert leads into paying clients by engaging in prospecting and lead generation as crucial parts of the sales process. This section will examine several approaches and methods for efficient lead generation and prospecting.

## Identifying Ideal Customer Profiles and Target Markets

Sales professionals must have a firm grasp on their target markets and ideal client profiles before beginning any prospecting efforts. This incorporates:

- Market Segmentation: Dividing the market into segments according to pertinent factors like age, location, industry verticals, and psychographic traits.

- Ideal Customer Profiles: The process of creating comprehensive profiles of ideal customers by considering various factors like industry, company size, job title, pain points, challenges, and purchasing behaviours.

- Value Proposition Alignment: Aligning the value proposition with the target market segments' needs, preferences, and pain points in order to ensure that the offered goods and services are closely aligned with them.

Sales representatives can concentrate their prospecting efforts on high-potential clients who are likely to benefit from their offers by determining target markets and ideal customer profiles.

## Methods for Prospecting: Cold Calling, Social Selling, Networking, and Referrals

Prospecting entails proactively locating and interacting with possible clients in order to start dialogues and cultivate connections. Typical methods for prospecting can include:

- Cold Calling: Making unsolicited phone calls to potential customers in order to introduce oneself, the business, and the offerings, as well as to determine the level of interest and qualify leads.

- Networking: Using contacts in the industry, decision-makers, influencers, and potential customers by utilising both personal and professional networks.

- Referrals: Reaching out to current clients, associates, and business associates to request introductions to other possible clients within their networks.

- Social Selling: interacting with clients and potential clients on social media sites like Facebook, LinkedIn, and Twitter in order to exchange useful content, create connections, and produce leads.

Sales professionals should test out various prospecting strategies to see which ones work best for their target markets and goals. Each prospecting strategy has benefits and drawbacks of its own.

## Leveraging Technology for Efficient Lead Generation

Thanks to technological advancements, sales professionals can now use a variety of tools and platforms to automate and streamline lead generation processes. This has completely changed how sales professionals prospect and generate leads. Several essential technologies and tactics consist of:

- Customer Relationship Management (CRM) Systems: Following up on leads, gathering information about prospects, and cultivating relationships over time are all made possible by using CRM systems.

- Marketing Automation: The implementation of marketing automation platforms is necessary to automate lead nurturing, email campaigns, follow-up procedures, and the tracking of prospect engagement and behaviour.

- Lead Generation Tools: Finding and obtaining leads from an array of online directories, social media platforms, and websites by utilising lead generation tools and software solutions.

- Data Analytics: Using predictive modelling and data analytics methods, high-potential leads are identified and ranked according to past trends, behaviours, and patterns.

Sales professionals can increase the efficacy of their lead generation processes, prospecting efforts, and lead identification and conversion processes by leveraging technology.

# Chapter 4: Effective Sales Presentations

Sales professionals can highlight their goods and services, respond to client needs, and influence potential customers to make purchases by using sales presentations, which are an essential part of the sales process. The essential elements of a successful sales presentation—preparation, delivery, dealing with objections, and using visual aids—will all be covered in this section.

# Crafting Strong Sales Presentations: Arrangement, Content, and Delivery

The first steps in creating a powerful sales presentation are preparation, which include:

- Understanding Customer Needs: Conducting research to gain insights into the prospect's industry, pain points, challenges, and objectives.

- Creating a Tailored Message: Adapting the presentation material to the particular requirements, passions, and concerns of the potential customer.

- Organizing the Presentation: Putting the presentation in order logically, beginning with a catchy opening and moving on to a summary of the agenda, important points, advantages, and a strong call to action.

- Creating Engaging Visuals: Using images to highlight important ideas, improve comprehension, and keep viewers interested, such as slides, graphs, charts, and videos.

- Practicing Delivery: Run through the presentation several times to make sure you can articulate yourself confidently, deliver the main points smoothly, and communicate them effectively.

Sales professionals can deliver presentations that resonate with prospects, address their needs, and ultimately lead to desired outcomes by devoting time and effort to preparation.

## Handling Objections and Overcoming Challenges During Presentations

It's not uncommon for prospects to voice reservations or objections regarding the offered good or service during sales presentations. Proactively addressing objections before they arise is a sign of an effective salesperson. Techniques for addressing objections consist of:

- Active Listening: Paying close attention to the prospect's worries without interjecting while exhibiting compassion and comprehension.

- Clarifying Concerns: Getting to the bottom of the objection by posing pointed questions that will help you understand its nature and its motivations.

- Offering Solutions: Presenting options or remedies to allay the prospect's worries and allay any apprehensions.

- Leveraging Social Proof: Presenting case studies, endorsements, success stories, and references to show the worth and legitimacy of the product.

- Resolving Price Concerns: Provide evidence of the product or service's features, advantages, and return on investment to support the price.

Salespeople can increase the possibility of a successful outcome by establishing rapport, trust, and credibility with prospects during presentations by skillfully handling objections and overcoming obstacles.

## Using Demonstrations and Visual Aids to Improve Communication

Using visual aids and demonstrations in sales presentations is an effective way to improve communication, grab the audience's attention, and reinforce important points. A few successful methods for utilising visual aids are as follows:

- Creating Compelling Slides: Crafting aesthetically pleasing slides that support important ideas and keep viewers interested through succinct text, sharp images, and understandable diagrams.

- Using Interactive Tools: Using interactive tools to demonstrate the capabilities of the offering and give hands-on experiences, such as product demos, simulations, and virtual tours.

- Demonstrating Value: Using graphics to highlight the special qualities, advantages, and value propositions of the good or service and set it apart from rivals.

- Introducing the Audience: Using surveys, tests, and interactive activities to promote audience participation and maintain their interest in the presentation.

Sales representatives may improve understanding, retention, and persuasion in their presentations and, eventually, close more deals by incorporating visual aids and demonstrations skillfully.

# Chapter 5: Negotiation Strategies and Closing Techniques

The last step in the sales process, closing a deal is frequently the most important one in obtaining a deal. Persuasion, skill, and knowledge of the needs and objections of the prospect are necessary. This section will examine different methods of closure and strategies for negotiating that salespeople can use to get the results they want.

## Understanding Different Closing Techniques: Trial Closes, Assumptive Closes, and More

Salespeople employ closing approaches to get a potential customer to decide what to buy. Typical methods for finishing a deal include:

- Trial Closes: Throughout the presentation, eliciting information from the prospect via statements or questions about their interest and willingness to buy. As an instance, "Would you prefer the standard package or the premium package?"

- Assumptive Closes: Making the assumption that the prospect has already made a purchase and framing inquiries in this manner. As an illustration, "When would you like delivery?"

- Urgency Closes: Stressing out the prospect with time-sensitive offers, discounts, or other incentives to get them to respond immediately.

- Summary Closes: providing a brief overview of the salient characteristics and advantages of the good or service and requesting the prospect's approval.

- Alternative Choice Closes: Giving the prospect a choice between two possibilities that earn a sale in each case. Such like "Would you like to proceed with the monthly subscription or the annual subscription?"

Salespeople can enhance their chances of completing a deal by learning and using several closing strategies, which allow them to modify their strategy according to the prospect's preferences and buying signals.

## Negotiation Strategies for Win-Win Outcomes

In order to create mutually advantageous agreements, negotiation is a crucial sales ability. Strategies for successful negotiations include:

- Readiness: Investigating the requirements, inclinations, and possible objections of the prospect in order to formulate a tactical plan before to engaging in talks.

- Active Listening: Active listening involves paying close attention to the worries, preferences, and goals of the prospect in order to find points of agreement and potential places for compromise.

- Value Proposition: Showcasing the special qualities and advantages of the product to support the price and show the prospect that it is a worthwhile investment.

- Creative Problem-Solving: Working together with the prospect to investigate possibilities or substitutes that satisfy their needs while resolving any roadblocks or difficulties.

- Maintaining Flexibility: Keeping an open mind and being willing to make compromises and concessions while being committed to reaching the agreed-upon goals and upholding the contract's integrity.

Salespeople may establish rapport, trust, and enduring connections with clients by approaching negotiations collaboratively and solution-focusedly, which will benefit both sides.

## Handling Price Objections and Negotiating Value

Salespeople frequently encounter price arguments, which can be difficult to overcome. Among the useful tactics for resolving concerns about pricing and negotiating value are:

- Value-Based Selling: Making the transition from price to value by highlighting the advantages, return on investment, and long-term worth of the product.

- ROI demonstration: Quantifying the value proposition by highlighting the possible revenue, cost savings, or efficiency advantages the prospect will realise from purchasing the good or service.

- Offering Alternatives: Providing substitute pricing, bundles, or payment schedules that satisfy the prospect's financial requirements without sacrificing quality.

- Addressing Concerns: Paying attention to the objections raised by the prospect and clearing up any misunderstandings or concerns regarding the cost, nature, or worth of the product.

Salespeople can increase the possibility of sealing the deal and satisfying both parties by skillfully handling pricing objections and negotiating value and developing trust, credibility, and confidence with prospects.

# Chapter 6: Sales Follow-Up and Customer Relationship Management

Building trust, fostering loyalty, and closing deals in the fast-paced world of sales all depend on efficient follow-up and customer relationship management (CRM). We will discuss the use of CRM systems, the significance of prompt and customised follow-up, and techniques for fostering enduring client relationships in this section.

## Importance of Effective Follow-Up in Sales: Timeliness, Personalization, and Persistence

In sales, it is essential to promptly follow up with prospects as it conveys professionalism, attentiveness, and dedication to their needs. Essential elements for successful follow-up consist of:

- Timeliness: To sustain momentum and keep the prospect interested, follow up as soon as possible following a sales presentation or initial point of contact.

- Personalisation: Adapting follow-up correspondence to each prospect's unique interests, concerns, and preferences in order to show that you are paying attention and to establish a rapport.

- Persistence: Staying in touch with prospects by sending them personalised messages, emails, and phone calls on a regular basis will help you stay top-of-mind and build a long-lasting relationship.

Salespeople can improve their responsiveness, credibility, and eventually their chances of turning leads into customers by emphasising prompt, customised, and persistent follow-up.

## Implementing CRM (Customer Relationship Management) Systems

CRM (customer relationship management) systems are strong instruments that help salespeople organise customer data, optimise interactions with prospects, and streamline business procedures. Important elements of CRM system implementation are as follows:

- Date Collection and Organisation: In order to obtain insights and customise communications, "Data Collection and Organisation" involves gathering and centralising customer data, such as contact details, interactions, preferences, and purchase history.

- Automated Workflows: Establishing automated workflows and reminders to guarantee timely and regular engagement for task assignments, follow-up activities, and communication scheduling.

- Analytics and Reporting: Utilising CRM's analytics and reporting capabilities to monitor sales results, gauge the success of campaigns, and pinpoint areas in need of development.

- Integration with Sales Tools: The process of integrating CRM systems with other sales tools and platforms, like email marketing software, lead generation tools, and customer support systems, can improve productivity and streamline workflows. This is known as **integration with sales tools**.

Sales professionals may streamline their workflows, increase productivity, and provide individualised experiences that foster customer loyalty by putting CRM systems into practice successfully.

# Building Long-Term Relationships for Repeat Business and Referrals

Establishing enduring connections with customers is crucial for cultivating allegiance, producing recurring business, and obtaining recommendations, even after the first sale. The following are some tactics for fostering lasting relationships:

- Continuous Communication: To stay in touch and provide continued value, keep in regular contact with clients by sending newsletters, updates, and customised messages.

- Value-Added Services: Improving the customer experience and strengthening relationships by providing value-added services like support, training, and special offers.

- Feedback and Engagement: Asking clients about their needs, preferences, and experiences; then, actively interacting with them to address any issues or recommendations.

- Reward and Recognition: Expressing gratitude and rewarding devoted clients with rewards, discounts, or unique rights in order to foster referrals and repeat business.

Sales professionals may develop brand ambassadors, spur revenue growth, and succeed in the long run in sales by placing a high priority on developing relationships and concentrating on providing outstanding customer experiences.

# Chapter 7: Sales Metrics and Performance Tracking

Tracking key performance indicators (KPIs) and analysing sales metrics are crucial for assessing performance, pinpointing areas for development, and achieving success in the fast-paced world of sales. The most important KPIs for sales success, methods for monitoring and evaluating sales data, and the application of data analytics to enhance sales performance are all covered in this part.

## Key Performance Indicators (KPIs) for Sales Success

Measurable measures known as key performance indicators (KPIs) are used to assess how successful and efficient sales efforts are. Among the most crucial KPIs for successful sales are:

- Conversion Rate: The proportion of leads or prospects who end up becoming actual customers by way of payment. A high conversion rate is a sign of successful lead nurturing and sales tactics.

- Sales Pipeline Velocity: The rate at which potential customers proceed from first contact to close in the sales pipeline.

Growing pipeline velocity is a sign of excellent lead management and efficient sales procedures.

- Average Deal Size: The mean amount of each transaction that the sales staff closes. Tracking average deal size makes it easier to spot patterns in the purchase habits of customers and prospective revenue.

- Win Rate: The proportion of prospects for sales that are converted into completed agreements. Strong sales performance and successful sales strategies are indicated by a high win rate.

- Customer Acquisition Cost (CAC): The average cost, including sales and marketing costs, of bringing on a new client. Tracking

CAC makes it easier to evaluate the effectiveness of marketing campaigns and the return on sales investments.

- Customer Lifetime Value (CLV): The total amount of money received from a client during the course of that client's association with the business. Growing CLV is a sign of effective customer loyalty and retention programmes.

Sales teams may evaluate their performance, pinpoint opportunities for development, and match their plans with organisational goals by monitoring these critical KPIs.

# Monitoring and Examining Sales Metrics: Revenue Growth, Sales Pipeline, and Conversion Rates

Monitoring a variety of sales indicators is necessary for effective sales tracking in order to assess performance and spot areas for improvement. Among the crucial sales indicators to monitor are:

- Conversion Rates: To find bottlenecks and streamline the sales process, track conversion rates at every point of the sales funnel, from lead generation to closing.

- Sales Pipeline: Predicting future income and setting priorities for sales activities by tracking prospects as they progress through the sales pipeline, including the quantity of leads, opportunities, and deals at each stage.

- Revenue Growth: Examining revenue patterns over time, such as growth rates from month to month and year to year, in order to evaluate sales results and pinpoint areas for growth.

- Sales Activity Metrics: Tracking phone calls, meetings, emails, and presentations to determine the efficiency and productivity of the sales staff.

Sales teams may enhance their performance, pinpoint areas for growth, and make data-driven decisions to propel revenue growth and success by routinely monitoring and evaluating key sales indicators.

## Maximizing Sales Performance using Data Analytics

Through the provision of actionable insights and the identification of improvement opportunities, data analytics plays a critical role in optimising sales performance. The following are some examples of how data analytics can be applied to improve sales performance:

- Predictive Analytics: Forecasting future sales patterns, identifying high-value prospects, and allocating resources optimally are all achieved by utilising past sales data and predictive models.

- Segmentation and Targeting: Using customer data analysis, divide the target audience into segments according to their preferences, behaviours, and demographics, then adjust sales tactics and messaging accordingly.

- Sales Forecasting: By utilising sales data and predictive analytics, sales teams can efficiently plan and prioritise their efforts by forecasting future revenue and setting realistic sales targets.

- Performance Benchmarking: Assessing areas of strength and weakness and benchmarking performance against industry standards by comparing sales performance data with competitors and industry benchmarks.

Sales teams may improve their strategy, understand consumer behaviour better, and generate profitable and sustainable development by utilising data analytics.

To sum up, in today's cutthroat business environment, successful sales metrics and performance tracking are critical for assessing sales performance, pinpointing areas for development, and fostering success. Sales teams can maximise productivity, spur revenue development, and accomplish business goals by concentrating on critical key performance indicators (KPIs), monitoring sales metrics, and utilising data analytics.

# Chapter 8: Continuous Learning and Professional Development

For sales professionals to succeed in their careers, maintain their competitiveness, and adjust to changing market conditions, they must pursue ongoing education and professional development. This section will address the value of spending money on professional development and training for salespeople, the advantages of networking and picking the brains of fellow salespeople and industry insiders, and methods for remaining current with best practices and market trends.

# Investing in Sales Training and Skill Development

For sales professionals, skill development and ongoing education are essential elements of their professional development. Purchasing sales training courses has a number of advantages, such as:

- Enhanced Sales Skills: Through sales training programmes, sales professionals can enhance their negotiation, objection-handling, and selling strategies, allowing them to function more productively in their positions.

- Product and Industry Knowledge: Product knowledge sessions and industry insights are frequently included in sales training programmes, providing sales professionals with the skills and information necessary to clearly communicate the value proposition of their offerings and successfully meet customer needs.

- Adaptability and Resilience: Sales training programmes encourage resilience and agility in navigating sales challenges by assisting sales professionals in adapting to shifting market dynamics, customer preferences, and competitive landscapes.

- Career Advancement: Ongoing education via sales training programmes boosts professional growth and creates doors for promotions to leadership positions and increased income potential in the sales industry.

Sales professionals can improve their skills, broaden their knowledge, and advance in their careers by investing in skill development and training.

## Networking and Learning from Sales Peers and Industry Experts

For sales professionals, networking and gaining knowledge from colleagues in the field as well as industry experts are invaluable sources of inspiration and knowledge. Developing connections with colleagues and business leaders has many advantages, such as:

- Knowledge Sharing: Sales professionals can benefit from each other's experiences and viewpoints by networking with peers in the industry and industry experts. This creates opportunities for idea exchange, collaborative problem-solving, and knowledge sharing.

- Professional Support: Establishing a robust network of sales contacts provides access to mentorship, professional support, and guidance from seasoned professionals who can provide insightful advice and guidance for overcoming obstacles in the sales field.

- Career Opportunities: Making connections with professionals in the field, building a profile within it, and opening doors to new collaborations and career prospects all contribute to the expansion of career opportunities through networking.

Sales professionals can effectively network and learn from peers and industry experts by participating in online communities, attending industry events, and joining professional organisations.

## Staying Updated on Market Trends and Best Practices

Remaining competitive and relevant in today's ever-evolving business environment requires sales professionals to stay up to date on market trends and best practices. Among the methods for keeping current are:

- Continuous Learning: Taking part in continuing professional development activities to stay up to date on new trends and best practices in sales, such as reading trade journals, going to webinars, and attending training sessions.

- Market Research: To identify market trends, customer preferences, and competitive dynamics, sales professionals should regularly conduct market research and competitor analysis. This will help them tailor their strategies and offerings to meet changing market demands.

- Networking and Collaboration: Making the most of networking opportunities to meet influential people in the field, go to conferences and events in the field, and work together with colleagues to exchange ideas and gain knowledge from one another's experiences.

Sales professionals can adjust their strategies, anticipate customer needs, and achieve success in their sales endeavours by staying abreast of market trends and best practices.

To sum up, in order for sales professionals to succeed in their careers, maintain their competitiveness, and adjust to shifting market conditions, they must engage in ongoing education and professional development. Sales professionals can improve their skills, widen their horizons, and succeed in the industry by investing in training and skill development, networking, learning from peers and industry experts, and staying current with market trends and best practices.

# Conclusion

To sum up, developing one's skills in sales is a complex process that calls for commitment, ongoing education, and methodical application. In order to achieve sales mastery and propel success in the cutthroat corporate world, we have examined a number of critical tactics and ideas throughout this book. While summarising the most important lessons learned and insights obtained, we also encourage continued study and application to advance your career and improve your sales performance.

## Key Sales Mastery Strategies Recap

1. Comprehending the Foundations: Starting with the basics, we discussed how important it is to define sales responsibilities, comprehend the sales process, and develop a mindset of confidence, resilience, and tenacity in order to succeed in sales.

2. Establishing Comradery and Connections: Successful sales interactions have been found to require the development of trust and the maintenance of solid connections with prospects and clients. In this sense, having strong communication skills, the capacity for attentive listening, and the capacity to develop value propositions that appeal to consumers are crucial.

3. Lead Generation and Prospecting: Key initiatives for filling the sales funnel and accelerating business growth included identifying ideal customer profiles, utilising a variety of prospecting techniques, and embracing technology for effective lead creation.

4. Making Strong Presentations: Careful planning, interesting material, and deft delivery are necessary for sales presentations to be effective. Dealing with objections and using visual aids to improve communication can have a big impact on how well sales presentations go.

5. Closing Methods and Strategies for Negotiation: In order to secure win-win

outcomes and successfully handle consumer objections, we investigated a variety of closing tactics and negotiation strategies. Successful transaction closure now requires the ability to handle pricing objections and negotiate value.

6. Customer relationship management and follow-up sales: Customer loyalty and repeat business can only be enhanced by deploying customer relationship management tools, prioritising long-term relationships, and following up with prospects and clients in a timely and personalised manner.

7. Achievement Metrics and Monitoring: In order to promote continuous improvement and meet sales targets, tracking KPIs, evaluating sales metrics, and utilising data

analytics to enhance sales performance have become essential procedures.

8. Lifelong Learning and Career Advancement: Finally, in order to succeed in the field of sales and maintain competitiveness, we stressed the significance of making investments in ongoing education, networking with colleagues and industry experts, and keeping up to current on best practices and market trends.

## Encouragement for Ongoing Learning and Implementation

I invite you to set out on a journey of continuous learning and application as you consider the tactics and insights offered in this book. Being a master of sales is a journey rather than a destination that requires constant improvement. You may successfully traverse the always changing sales market by adopting an attitude of curiosity, adaptability, and resilience.

To further hone your talents, try out new strategies, get input from mentors and peers, and incorporate the concepts and tactics you've learned here into your everyday sales operations. Take the initiative to look for chances for professional growth, whether they come from official training courses, trade shows, or casual networking.

Above all, continue to be passionate about quality and dedicated to providing value to your consumers and clients. You may realise your greatest potential as a sales professional and have a career of unmatched success by adopting these traits and embracing a lifelong learning and development path.

Finally, I hope that your path to sales expertise continues to be fruitful. May you rise to new heights in your pursuit of excellence, embrace the challenges, and enjoy the successes.